Last Words from Texas

Last Words from Texas

Meditations from the Execution Chamber

Rev. Dr. Jeff Hood

WIPF & STOCK · Eugene, Oregon

Cover Painting: "The Witness of the Masses" by Emily Hood

For Sister Helen Prejean,
who first engaged my heart on the death penalty

For Major Kathy Cox,
who showed me what a heart for those on death row looks like

For Kim Jackson,
who helped to expand my heart to those abolitionists who
don't even know what that word means

In February of 2015, I started a long journey of meditation. For over 42 days, I prayed the last words of 84 men and women who have been executed in Texas. Based on my morning and evening meditations, I created these 84 devotional reflections.

TEXAS

#1 Charlie Brooks, Jr. / December 7, 1982

"Be strong."

As a devout Muslim, Charlie Brooks, Jr. firmly believed that this life was only for the purpose of preparing for the life that is to come. Brooks wanted his family and friends to be strong in the face of injustice and oppression. No matter what we call God, I believe that God's message from the next life to us is always, "Be strong." Can you hear the voice of God encouraging you to be strong?

I invite you to pray the last words of Charlie Brooks, Jr. as if you are hearing them directly from God:

"Be strong."

Amen.

#2 James Autry / March 14, 1984

Silence.

James Autry declined to give any last words. Sometimes, God is found most clearly in the silence. I believe that Autry heard the voice of a loving God calling him home in those final moments. In the silence, have you ever heard the voice of God?

I invite you to experience the lack of last words from James Autry:

Silence.

Amen.

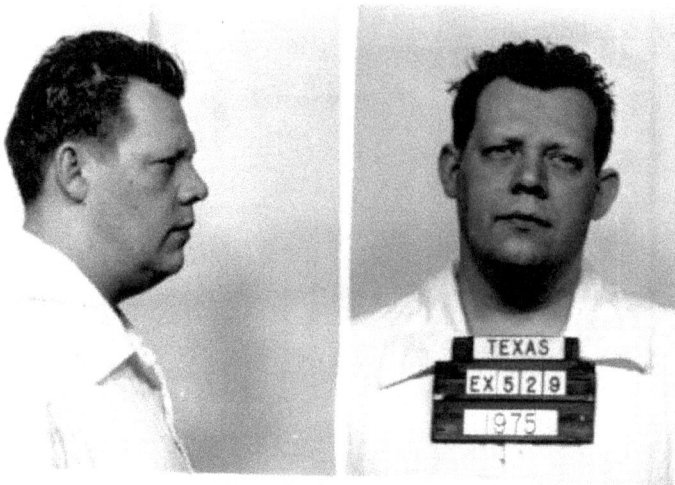

#3 Ronald Clark O'Bryan / March 30, 1984

"What is about to transpire in a few moments is wrong!"

Throughout life, there are times when we feel helpless about the evil that is raging around us. In these moments, I believe that we are called to do the only thing that we can do and name what is happening. Ronald Clark O'Bryan was about to be executed and he knew that it was wrong for the State of Texas to take his life. In naming the evil, O'Bryan bore witness to the evil that was and provided a dissenting voice that has been carried into the future. Have you ever prayed for the courage to name evil when you cannot change it?

I invite you to pray the last words of Ronald Clark O'Bryan in anticipation of moments of helplessness in the face of evil:

"What is about to transpire in a few moments is wrong!"

Amen.

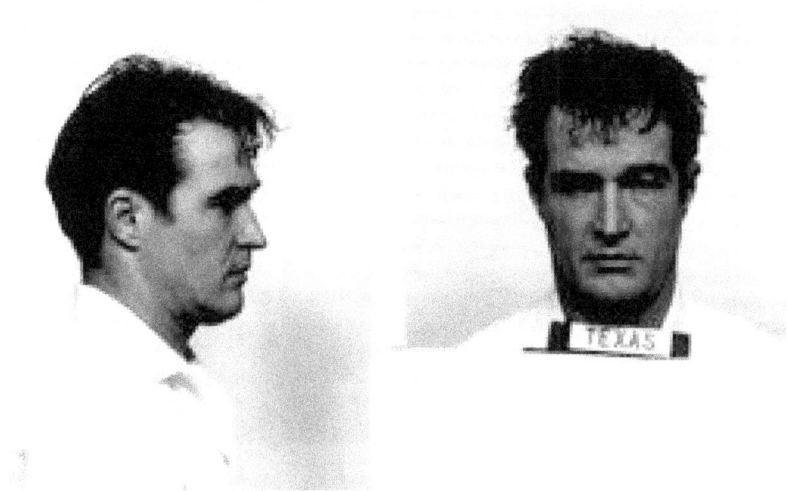

#4 Thomas Barefoot / October 30, 1984

"I want everybody to know that I hold nothing against them."

How often do we go through life holding grudges? Thomas Barefoot wanted everyone to know that he was not leaving earth with any grudges. What if we lived life without holding grudges? Surely, God can help us excise the grudges that we carry.

I invite you to pray the last words of Thomas Barefoot until they are reality:

"I want everybody to know that I hold nothing against them."

Amen.

#5 Doyle Skillern / January 16, 1985

"I pray that my family will rejoice..."

What is there to rejoice about in death? Our culture spends so
much time trying to convince each of us that death is not
coming. We try with all that we are to reject aging and death.
Doyle Skillern used his final words to encourage his family to
rejoice in his life and his completion of the journey. Believing
that what lied ahead had to be better, Skillern didn't want
anybody to weep for him. What would it look like if we
anticipated the day of our death with hope instead of dread?

I invite you to pray the last words of Doyle Skillern:

"I pray that my family will rejoice..."

Amen.

#6 Stephen Morin / March 13, 1985

"I give thanks for this time..."

Our lives are most full when we are able to be thankful no matter the circumstance. Stephen Morin wanted to give thanks for the time to speak while he was laying on the gurney in the execution chamber. What is your excuse for giving thanks?

I invite you to pray the last words of Stephen Morin:

"I give thanks for this time."

Amen.

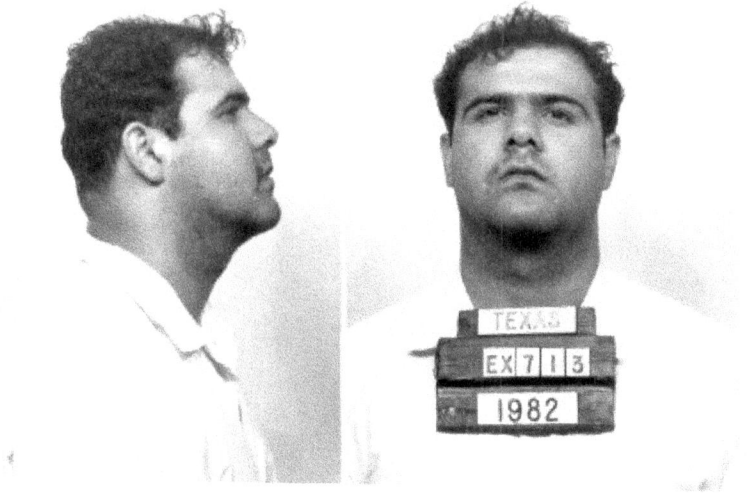

#7 Jesse De La Rosa / May 15, 1985

Silence.

Why do we consistently silence people? In the face of execution, Jesse De La Rosa chose not to say a word. Why did we put him in a lethal situation where he had to choose? In the silence of De La Rosa, is the loud indictment of our silence.

In the silence of De La Rosa, I invite you to pray silently for the courage to speak:

Silence.

Amen.

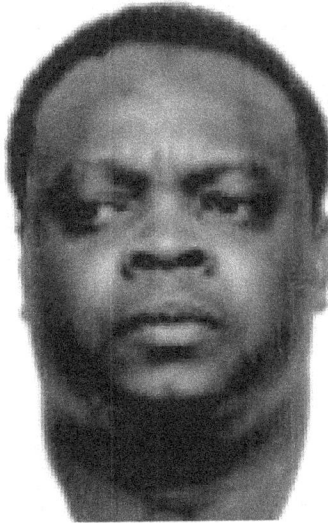

#8 Charles Milton / June 25, 1985

"There's no God but Allah..."

For a long time, I feared that statements about Allah were heresy and antithetical to my Christian beliefs. After developing numerous close friendships with Muslims, I don't believe that any more. I read the last words of Charles Milton to say, "There is no God but God." Regardless, Milton affirmed his belief in Allah or God in his final words. What would it look like for us to use the word God interchangeably with the word Allah?

In solidarity with the Islamic peoples of our planet, I invite you to pray the last words of Charles Milton:

"There's no God but Allah..."

Amen.

#9 Henry Porter / July 9, 1985

"A Mexican's life is worth nothing."

Before his execution, Henry Porter spoke truth to power. Since Porter spoke these words, Mexicans have consistently died in the violence of their country or trying to flee and cross our borders. We don't care. The only thing that matters to us is protecting our vast wealth. We are a greedy people. Is a Mexican's life worth anything in this country?

As a means of confession and as a way to work toward a world were the lives of Mexicans matter just as much as our lives, I invite you to pray the last words of Henry Porter:

"A Mexican's life is worth nothing."

Amen.

#10 Charles Rumbaugh / September 11, 1985

"I am ready to begin my journey..."

Charles Rumbaugh believed that death was a journey. When I read these words, I thought that we being the journey of death when we are born. I think there was a reason that Rumbaugh didn't speak to where the journey ends. Perhaps, the journey never ends and we keep dying into love. Maybe, this is the message of God. Are you ready to begin your journey?

I invite you to pray the last words of Charles Rumbaugh:

"I am ready to begin my journey..."

Amen.

#11 Charles Bass / April 12, 1986

"I deserve this."

There are times in our lives that we feel so burdened by guilt that we believe that we deserve whatever punishment may come. In such moments, Jesus extends a punishment that is lighter than anything we could ever imagine. What we deserve is death, but Jesus extends grace to us in the form of everlasting love. We were made for love. We deserve love.

With love in mind, I invite you to pray the last words of Charles Bass:

"I deserve this."

Amen.

#12 Jeffery Barney / April 16, 1986

Silence.

Jeffery Barney declined to make a last statement. In his final breaths, Barney said nothing. Maybe with his breath, Barney said everything. Perhaps, Barney affirmed that each of his breaths belonged to God and that it was God who was going to decide when they stop.

In the silence of Jeffery Barney, I invite you to affirm whom your breaths belong to:

Silence.

Amen.

#13 Jay Pinkerton / May 15, 1986

"I love you, Dad"

There is something transcendent about proclaiming love. In his final words, Jay Pinkerton wanted his dad to know that he loved him. How many of us can relate to a desire to proclaim love? Sometimes we are invited to proclaim love in order to bring love into a loveless void.

Regardless of whether your relationship with your father is good or bad, I invite you to pray the last words of Jay Pinkerton:

"I love you, Dad"

Amen.

#14 Rudy Ramos Esquivel / June 9, 1986

"...be cool."

I have always thought that someone is cool when they are able to be. With his last words, Rudy Ramos Esquivel encouraged everyone to be cool or to simply be. Simply being in a word of imposters is quite the achievement. There is so much pressure to be anything other than true to your self. With the life about to be taken out of his body, Esquivel encouraged everyone who could hear to be.

In the midst of an anxious world, I invite you to pray the last words of Rudy Ramos Esquivel:

"...be cool."

Amen.

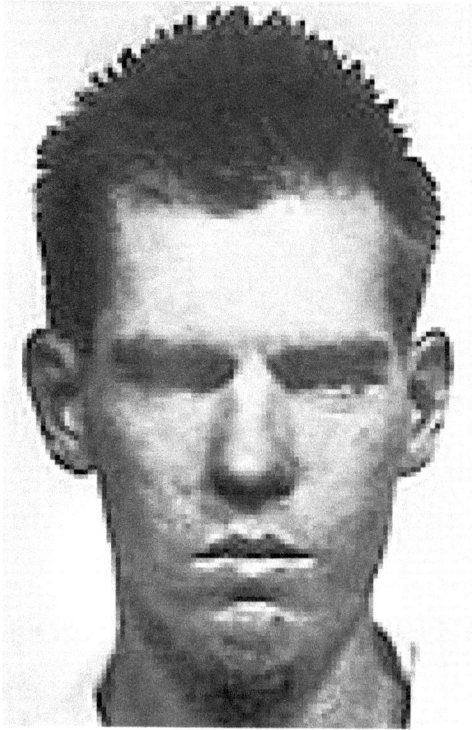

#15 Kenneth Brock / June 19, 1986

"I am ready."

We spend so much time worrying about everything. In the face of death, Kenneth Brock was at ease. What would it be like for us to meet every moment and stage of live ready?

I invite you to pray the last words of Kenneth Brock:

"I am ready."

Amen.

#16 Randy Woolls / August 20, 1986

"I want those out there to keep fighting the death penalty."

The modern movement to abolish the death penalty is full of vibrant and intelligent people. Randy Woolls wanted to encourage abolitionists to keep fighting. What are you fighting for? Would someone spend their last words encouraging you to keep going?

With deep thought about what you are going to give your life to, I invite you to pray the last words of Randy Woolls:

"I want those out there to keep fighting the death penalty."

Amen.

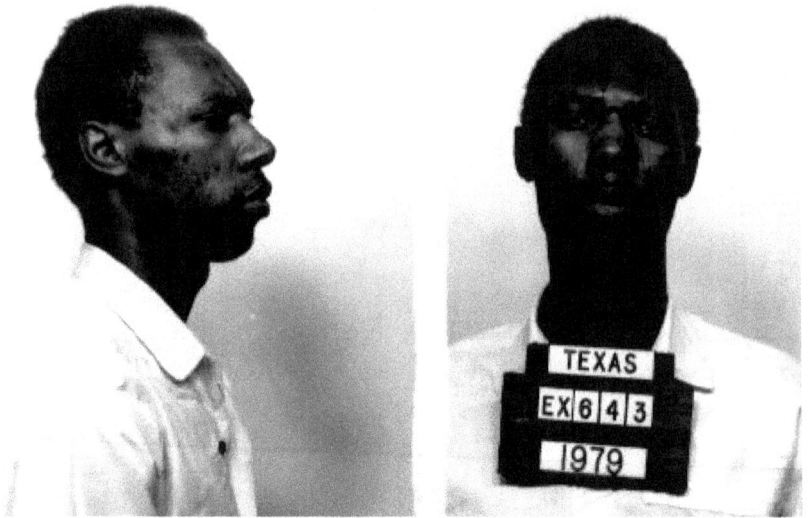

#17 Larry Smith / August 22, 1986

"God bless her."

Who are the women in you life that you would ask God to bless with your last words? Larry Smith chose to ask God to bless his mother. We should follow Smith's example and think about women that we should ask God to bless. Who are the important women in your life?

Thinking about the women who have made a difference in your life, I invite you to pray the last words of Larry Smith:

"God bless her."

Amen.

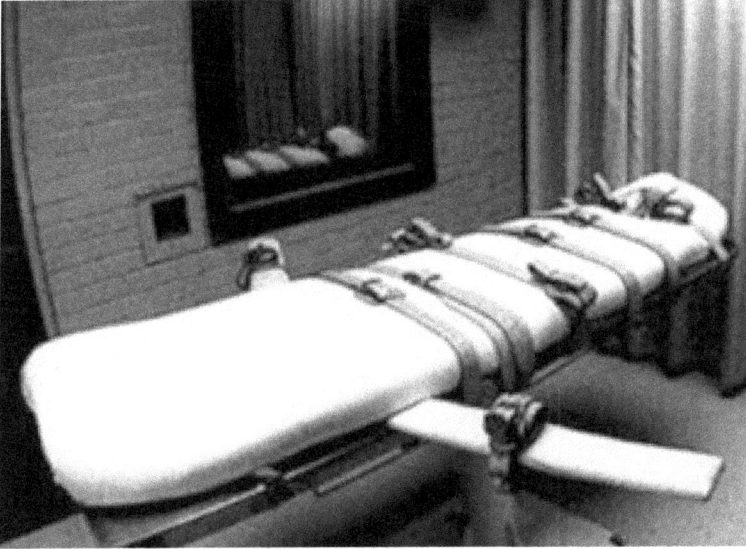

#18 Chester Wicker / August 26, 1986

Silence.

Chester Wicker remained silent throughout his execution.

With the silence of Chester Wicker in mind, I invite you to experience:

Silence.

Amen.

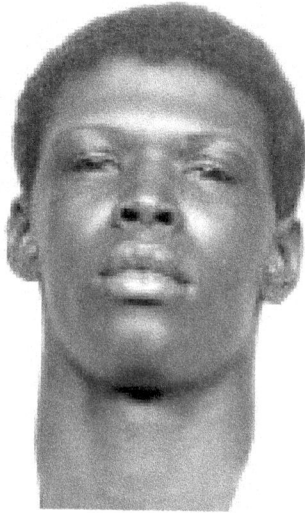

#19 Michael Evans / December 4, 1986

"...I hope I'm forgiven."

The writer of Hebrews declared, "Faith is the assurance of things hoped for..." Hope is a beautiful thing that creates beautiful realities in the economy of God. We hope in order to survive. We hope in order to declare our future. When Michael Evans declared "...I hope I am forgiven," he should have considered it done in the eyes of God. We too can live with such a hope.

I invite you to pray the last words of Michael Evans with the great reality that is hope:

"...I hope I'm forgiven."

Amen.

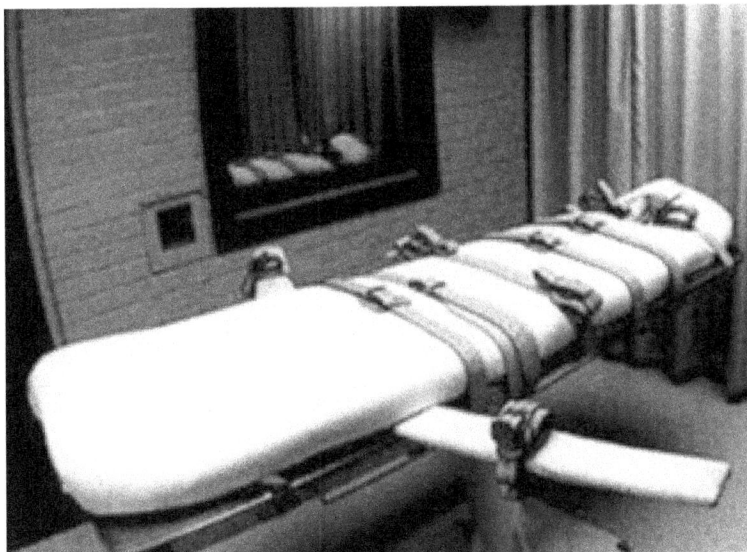

#20 Richard Andrade / December 18, 1986

Silence.

Richard Andrade declined to give a final statement. All that Andrade could hear in the chamber was his breath. Do you ever listen for your breath?

In the spirit of Richard Andrade, I invite you to pray as you listen for your breath in the:

Silence.

Amen.

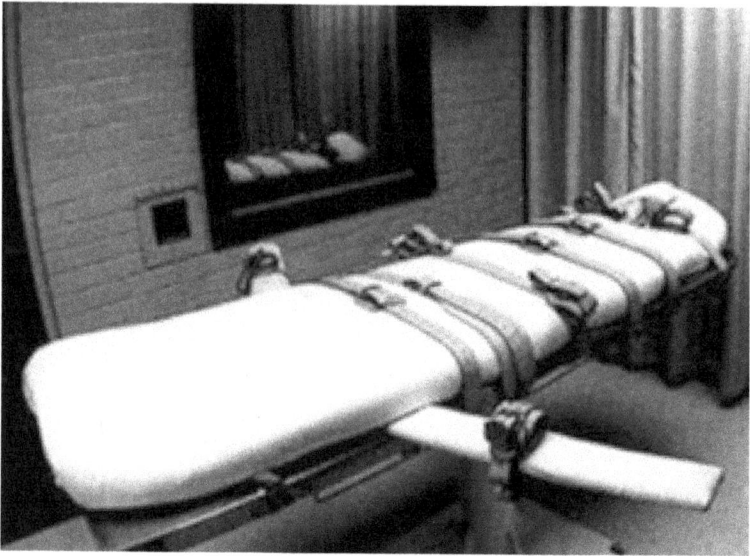

#21 Ramon Hernandez / January 30, 1987

Silence.

Ramon Hernandez did not speak. Are there ever times when you should have spoken and you chose to remain silent?

I invite you to engage the silence of the execution of Ramon Hernandez and think about when you should speak in this moment of:

Silence.

Amen.

#22 Eliseo Moreno / March 4, 1987

Silence.

Can you imagine what it is like to not be heard? Perhaps, the silence of Eliseo Moreno was his resignation to the fact that his voice would not be heard. What can we do to make sure that all voices are heard?

I invite you to engage the silence of Eliseo Moreno and ponder what you can do to lift up the voices of the silenced:

Silence.

Amen.

#23 Anthony Williams / May 28, 1987

"...watch out for the family."

How expansive is your definition of family? Most people think
that family includes only their immediate family and maybe
some extended family. What if we were bold enough to believe
that the whole world is our family? Anthony Williams asked a
couple of people to watch out for what he considered to be his
family. What if we took Anthony's challenge and watched out
for the whole world?

I invite you to pray the last words of Anthony Williams:

"...watch out for the family."

Amen.

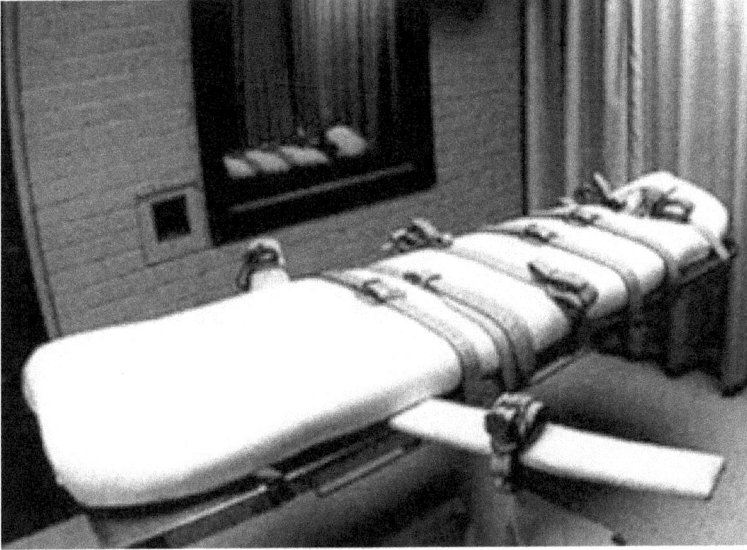

#24 Elliot Johnson / June 24, 1987

Silence.

Elliot Johnson declined to make a statement.

I invite you to address the void that Johnson left:

Silence.

Amen.

TEXAS

#25 John Thompson / July 8, 1987

Silence.

John Thompson declined to make a statement.

I invite you to address the void that Thompson left:

Silence.

Amen.

#26 Joseph Starvaggi / September 10, 1987

Silence.

Joseph Starvaggi declined to make a statement.

I invite you to address the void that Starvaggi left:

Silence.

Amen.

#27 Robert Streetman / January 7, 1988

Silence.

Robert Streetman declined to make a statement.

I invite you to address the void that Streetman left:

Silence.

Amen.

#28 Donald Franklin / November 3, 1988

Silence.

Donald Franklin declined to make a statement.

I invite you to address the void that Franklin left:

Silence.

Amen.

#29 Raymond Landry, Sr. / December 13, 1988

Silence.

Raymond Landry, Sr. declined to make a statement.

I invite you to address the void that Landry left:

Silence.

Amen.

#30 Leon King / March 22, 1989

"I love you all."

When it is my time to go, I pray that I will leave this world with nothing but love in my heart for everyone. Leon King wanted everyone to know that he loved them. I think Jesus was the same way. Despite the agony of the cross, Jesus tried to love and forgive until the very end. I don't think we have to wait until the end to start working toward a universal love. Do you?

I invite you to pray the last words of Leon King:

"I love you all."

Amen.

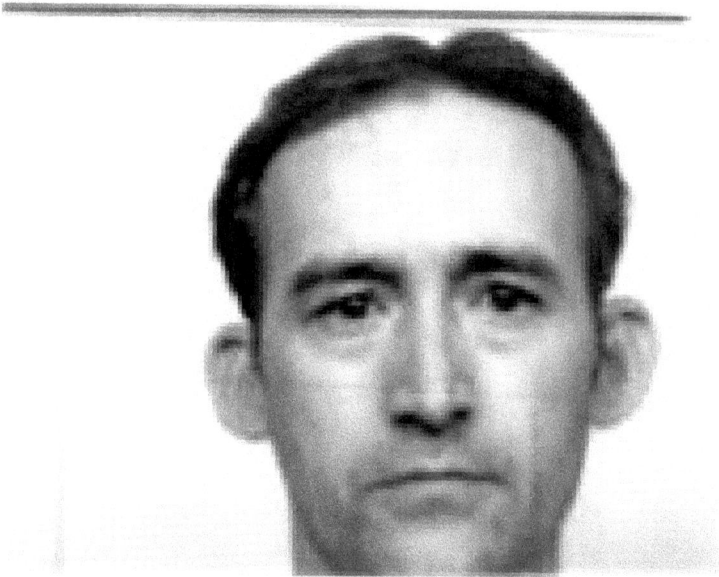

#31 Stephen McCoy / May 24, 1989

Silence.

Stephen McCoy declined to make a statement.

I invite you to address the void that Stephen left:

Silence.

Amen.

#32 James Paster / September 20, 1989

"I hope...can find peace in this."

In the terrifying and painful confusion of the final moments of his execution, James Paster wanted his death to bring peace to someone who was suffering. What is peace? Is peace the absence of fighting? Is peace a destination or a place? Is peace the absence of suffering? While some of these questions might make good definitions, I think the peace that is most pertinent to this situation is about finding God in what is. What can you do to help people find God in the terror and pain of their lives?

Thinking of how your life can help bring peace to those around you, I invite you to pray the last words of James Paster:

"I hope...can find peace in this."

Amen.

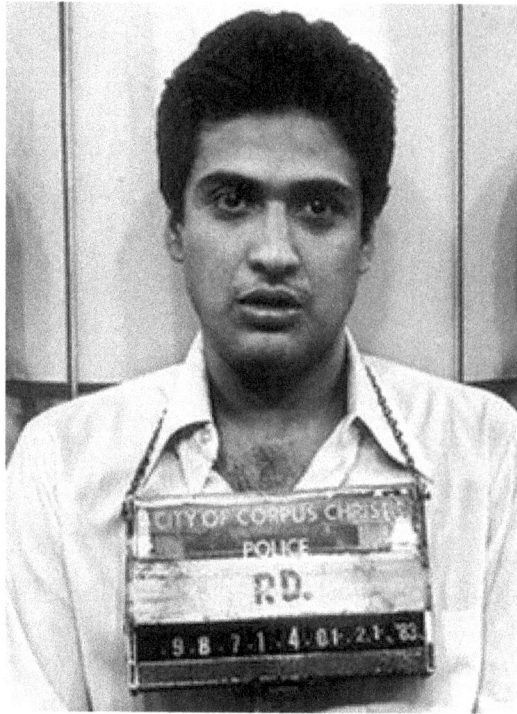

#33 Carlos DeLuna / December 7, 1989

"...keep the faith and don't give up."

Can you imagine being about to die and your chief concern is the fortitude of others? Though Carlos DeLuna was speaking to the folks on death row, I believe he just as well was speaking to us.

I invite you to pray the last words of Carlos DeLuna:

"...keep the faith and don't give up."

Amen.

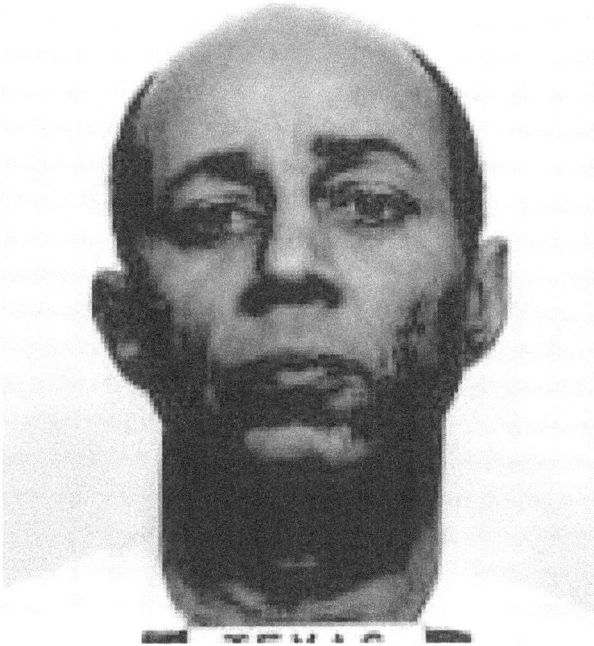

#34 Jerome Butler / April 21, 1990

"Everything is OK"

In the confusion of life, it is easy to become terrorized by all that surrounds us. In his final moments, Jerome Butler had every reason to be terrified. With his final words, Butler pushed back and declared everything to be OK. If Butler could find words of calm in the terror, why do we live so terrified?

I invite you to pray the last words of Jerome Butler:

"Everything is OK"

Amen.

#35 Johnny Anderson / May 17, 1990

"I still proclaim I am innocent..."

If we don't believe that we are innocent then who will? For me, innocence is not as much about whether someone committed a crime or not as it is about believing that someone still has intrinsic value and worth despite their crimes. Though Johnny Anderson was speaking about his case, what would it be like if we repeated his assertion in our lives on a daily basis?

I invite you to pray the last words of Johnny Anderson:

"I still proclaim I am innocent..."

Amen.

#36 James Smith / June 26, 1990

Silence.

James Smith declined to make a statement.

I invite you to address the void that James left:

Silence.

Amen.

#37 Mikel Derrick / July 18, 1990

"...just forgive me..."

We all mess up. We all make mistakes. Mikel Derrick is not all that different from any of the rest of us. In the midst of death, Derrick just wanted forgiveness. Why are we so hesitant to ask for forgiveness? Why does it often take death to awaken us?

Facing the world, I invite you to pray the last words of Mikel Derrick:

"...just forgive me..."

Amen.

#38 Lawrence Buxton / February 26, 1991

"I'm ready..."

People are able to start trips with confidence when they know where they are going. When his time was forced upon him, Lawrence Buxton confidently declared his readiness to start the journey into death. How will we respond when our time comes? Will we have the confidence of knowing where we are going?

With less of a thought about the timing and more of a thought about the destination, I invite you to pray the last words of Lawrence Buxton:

"I'm ready..."

Amen.

#39 Ignacio Cuevas / May 23, 1991

"I'm going to a beautiful place."

Where are you going? Ignacio Cuevas knew that something greater was coming. How different would life be if we all lived with such confidence?

I invite you to pray the last words of Ignacio Cuevas:

"I'm going to a beautiful place."

Amen.

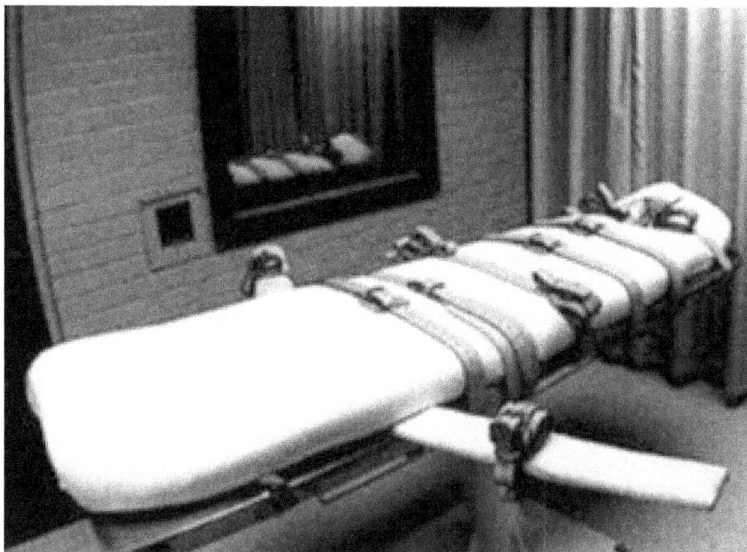

#40 Jerry Bird / June 17, 1991

"Start things rolling."

Though some are going sooner than others, we are all dying. In the face of his death, Jerry Bird wanted to get things rolling. Oddly, Bird showed tremendous agency and life by demanding that his execution start. Will you sit and wait for death or start to be an active participant in life?

I invite you to pray the last words of Jerry Bird:

"Start things rolling."

Amen.

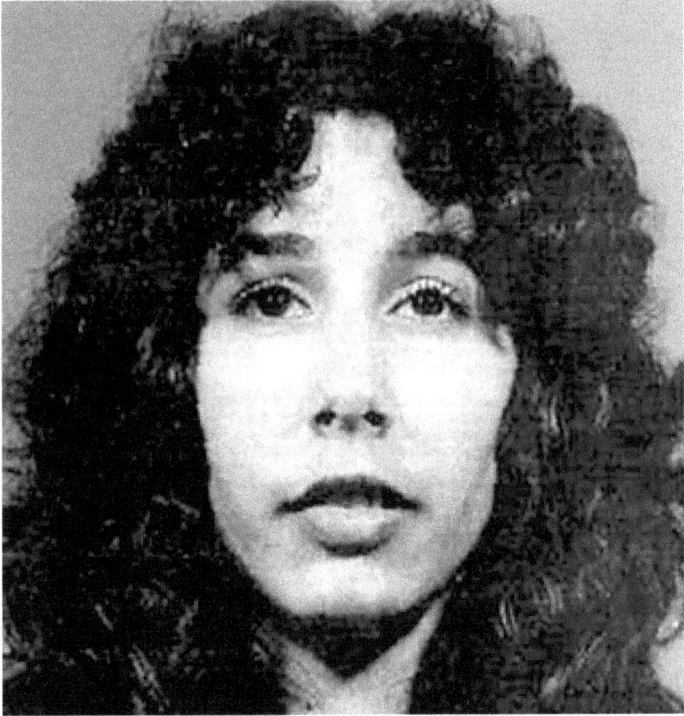

#145 Karla Faye Tucker / February 3, 1998

"I will wait for you."

Everyone is trying to get ahead. No one wants to wait. In her final moments, Karla Faye Tucker told all who would listen that she would wait for them. Maybe there is still value in waiting on others.

I invite you to pray the last words of Karla Faye Tucker:

"I will wait for you."

Amen.

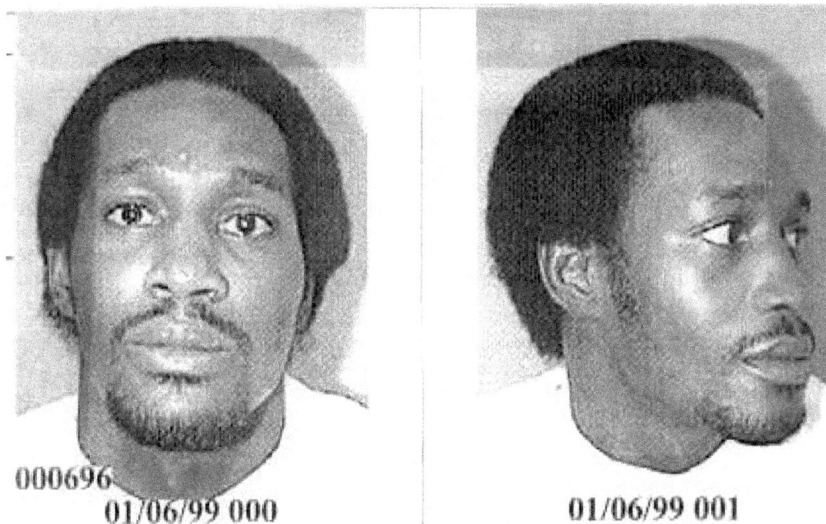

01/06/99 000

01/06/99 001

000696

#222 Shaka Sankofa aka Gary Graham / June 22, 2000

"But they cannot acknowledge my innocence, because to do so would be to publicly admit their guilt."

We have a difficult time believing that there is anything innocent in our enemies. To acknowledge innocence in our enemies would be to acknowledge guilt in our self. Maybe it is better to approach people and the world as both innocent and guilty. In his final moments, Shaka Sankofa reminded us that innocence and guilt are inextricably linked together.

I invite you to pray the last words of Shaka Sankofa:

"But they cannot acknowledge my innocence, because to do so would be to publicly admit their guilt."

Amen.

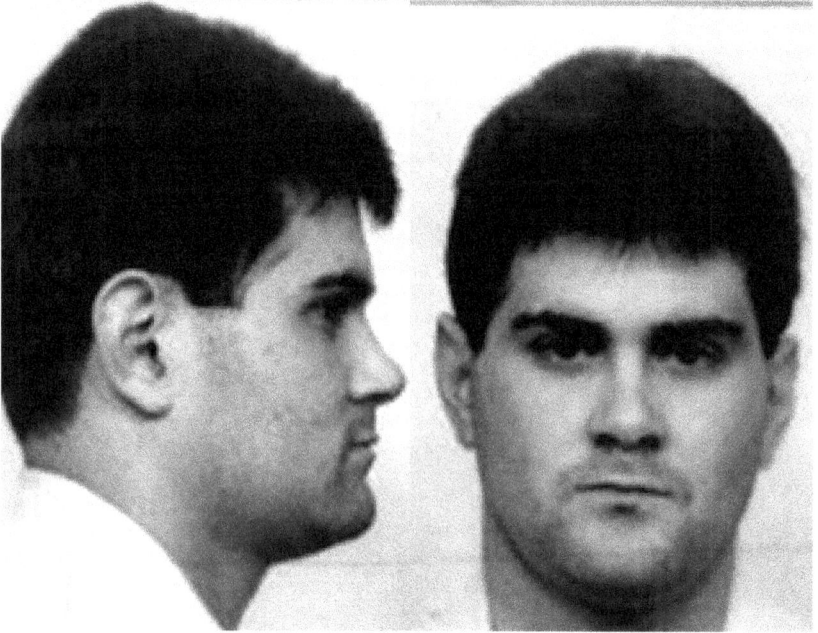

#320 Cameron Todd Willingham / February 17, 2004

"From God's dust I came and to dust I will return - so the earth
shall become my throne."

We forget that we are dust. We forget that we will return to
dust. Cameron Todd Willingham realized that in the dust is life
and in life is dust. How do you encounter your dust?

I invite you to pray the last words of Cameron Todd
Willingham:

"From God's dust I came and to dust I will return - so the earth
shall become my throne."

Amen.

#483 Yokamon Hearn / July 18, 2012

"I wish ya'll well."

There is something very spiritual about wishing other people well. Yokamon Hearn wanted his final moments to be filled with love for others. How do you wish to fill your moments?

I invite you to pray the last words of Yokamon Hearn:

"I wish ya'll well."

Amen.

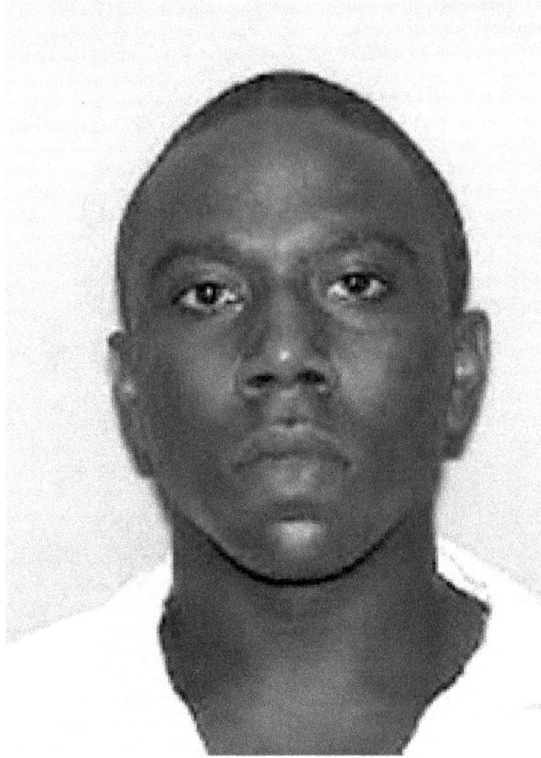

#483 Beunka Adams / April 26, 2012

"Murder isn't right."

We don't have to kill people. Why do we keep killing? Let's
pray that we stop.

I invite you to pray the last words of Beunka Adams:

"Murder isn't right."

Amen.

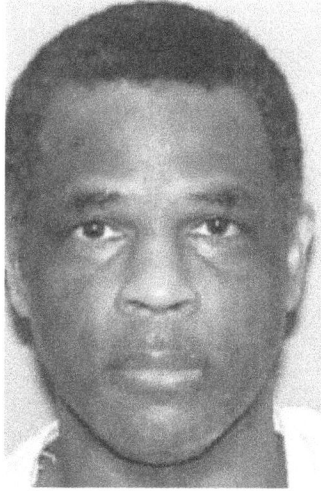

#484 Marvin Wilson / August 7, 2012

"Ya'll do understand that I came here a sinner and leaving a saint."

In his final moments, Marvin Wilson wanted the room to know that he was a redeemed child of God. In the midst of a world that called him a criminal and a sinner, Wilson still found his way to God. Sometimes in the midst of a world that so desperately wants to nail us to the wall with our past mistakes, we have to push toward where we are going and not dwell on where we have been. The lesson that Wilson left us with is that all of us can be a saint if we want to. Do you want to?

I invite you to pray the last words of Marvin Wilson:

"Ya'll do understand that I came here a sinner and leaving a saint."

Amen.

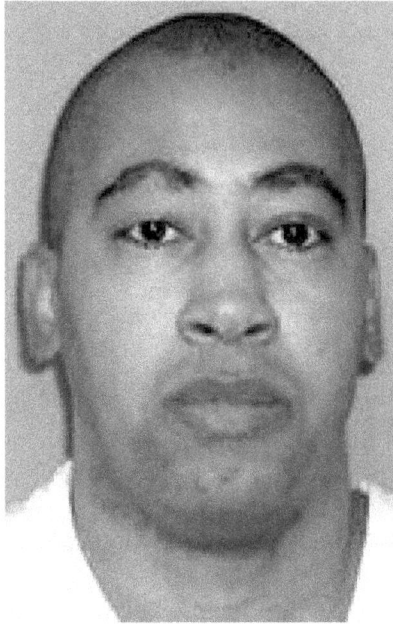

#485 Robert Wayne Harris / September 20, 2012

"I'm going home, I'm going home. I'll be alright, don't worry."

Robert Wayne Harris wanted everyone to be at ease as he finished his journey. In John 14:1, Jesus speaks to the disciples in the same way, "Let not your hearts be troubled..." Though there was still pain and suffering to face, Jesus knew that he was going home. What if we lived as if we were just on our way home?

I invite you to pray the last words of Robert Wayne Harris:

"I'm going home, I'm going home. I'll be alright, don't worry."

Amen.

#486 Cleve Foster / September 25, 2012

"Over the years I have learned to love."

When Cleve Foster was about to die, he wanted everyone to know that he had learned to love. Sometimes love takes some growing into. We live in a cruel world and love seems to be a precious and endangered commodity. Often, people just learn to live and survive by being just as heartless as everyone else. Cleve wanted to live differently and worked hard to learn to love. The God who is love wants us all to learn to love. How are your love studies coming along?

With great expectation for what God can and will do in your life, I invite you to pray the last words of Cleve Foster:

"Over the years I have learned to love."

Amen.

#487 Jonathan Green / October 10, 2012

"It hurts bad."

In his final moments, Jonathan Green wanted to give voice to the pain that he was suffering. On the cross, Jesus screamed out in pain, "My God, My God, Why have you forsaken me?" In the midst of our pain, why do we feel the need to go through life silent about it? We make life all the more torturous by not naming the pain. Tell people that it hurts. Remember, God is with the hurting.

I invite you to pray the last words of Jonathan Green:

"It hurts bad."

Amen.

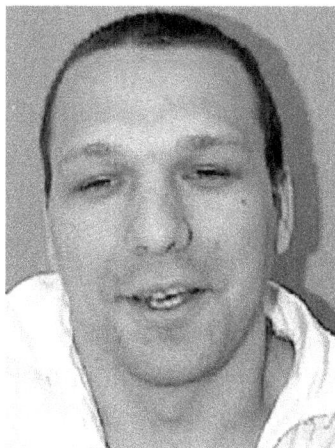

#488 Bobby Lee Hines / October 24, 2012

"Please forgive me."

Forgiveness is a powerful phenomenon that can set both the offender and the offended free. Shortly before he was executed, Bobby Lee Hines asked for forgiveness. While it is impossible to know if Bobby was forgiven by those associated with his crimes or not, we can only know that God generously forgives all who ask for forgiveness and we are taught to do the same. In Luke 6:37, Jesus also says, "If you forgive others, you will be forgiven." We are called to forgive all who seek forgiveness. If we dare forgive others, perhaps we might be able to forgive the most horrible sinner of all...our self. Do you have the courage to engage in radical forgiveness?

I invite you to pray the last words of Bobby Lee Hines,

"Please forgive me."

Amen.

#489 Donnie Lee Roberts, Jr. / October 31, 2012

Donnie Lee Roberts, Jr.-

"God knows I didn't want to do what I did."

If we allow it, evil can possess and overtake over our lives. Upon possession, we do not necessarily do the things that we want to do. In his final moments, Donnie Lee Roberts, Jr. wanted the world to know that he didn't want to kill anyone. I believe him. There have been times in my life that I let evil in and didn't necessarily do the things that I wanted to do. Can you think of moments in your life where you didn't want to do the evil things that you did? God knows we wanted to do better and stands ready to forgive us.

I invite you to pray the last words of Donnie Lee Roberts, Jr. as a means of release and request for forgiveness,

"God knows I didn't want to do what I did."

Amen.

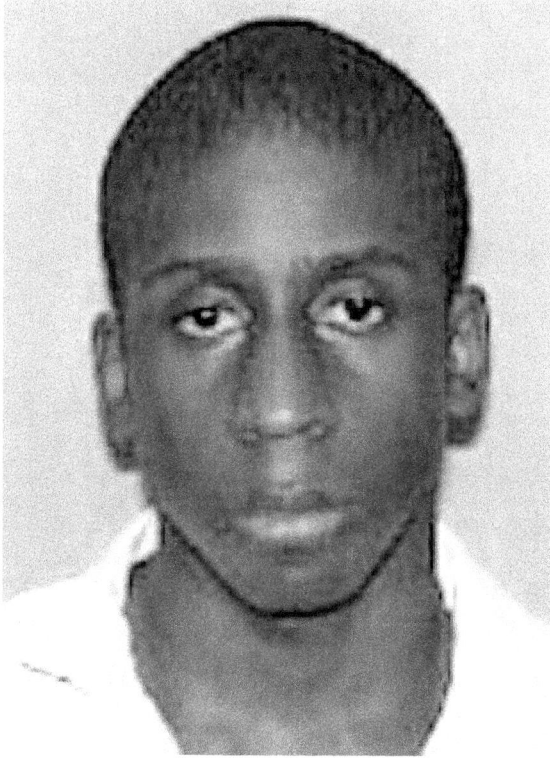

#490 Mario Swain / November 8, 2012

Silence.

Mario Swain offered no words when he was executed. Why didn't we speak up to save him?

I invite you to spend a few moments pondering the silence of Mario Swain:

Silence.

Amen.

#491 Ramon Torres Hernandez / November 14, 2012

"Can you hear me?"

Before Ramon Torres Hernandez was executed, he wanted to know if anyone could hear him. I cannot count the late nights of prayer where I have laid awake pondering whether I was heard. Is God real? I don't have robust proof. There are moments where I think I know and there are moments where I know I don't. Regardless of my confused thoughts, I can only tell you that for some strange compelling reason I keep talking to whatever is out there. Maybe every step of faith begins with having the courage to ask if anything is there to listen?

I invite you to pray the last words of Ramon Torres Hernandez:

"Can you hear me?"

Amen.

#492 Preston Hughes / November 15, 2012

"...fight for my innocence..."

Have you ever been falsely accused of something? Until the very end, Preston Hughes maintained he was innocent. Even in death, Hughes wanted his family to fight for his innocence and clear his name. Regardless of the veracity of his claims, I believe that we all begin innocent. Unfortunately, there is an accuser out there who constantly wants us to believe that we are guilty and condemned. Hughes refused to believe the accusations and fought for his innocence. I wish we would have the courage to fight back against the accusations and start living into the person God created us to be. No matter what has happened, you started innocent and pure...go back there. Do you have the courage to fight for your innocence?

Thinking of both yourself and those who love you, I invite you to pray the last words of Preston Hughes:

"...fight for my innocence..."

Amen.

#493 Carl Blue / February 21, 2013

"We all have to die to get to heaven."

When I think about heaven, I think about the overwhelming and intoxicating embrace of love. Sometimes, I think we get glimpses of extravagant love on earth. Regardless of when we are talking, I don't think love comes without death. We have to die to our self in order to be able to love anything else. We have to die to our self in order to experience the full love of God. Carl Blue knew about love and wanted to share his knowledge of love in his final moments. Love won in his life and love will win in all of our lives if we stop holding on to the illusions of control and embrace the limitless power of love.

I invite you to pray the last words of Carl Blue:

"We all have to die to get to heaven."

Amen.

#494 Ricky Lewis / April 9, 2013

"It's burning."

When the poison started to flow through the needle, Ricky Lewis said that his body was burning. Lewis is just one example of a great many executed persons who have reported a burning sensation before they died. Though the burning is used to argue that the execution process is a violation of the constitutional protection against cruel and unusual punishment, I am hungry for the day when we realize that killing people is always evil. Shall we light the fire and let our bodies burn boldly with love for all of God's children?

With the idea that the fire of love can save us from all this killing, I invite you to pray the last words of Ricky Lewis:

"It's burning."

Amen.

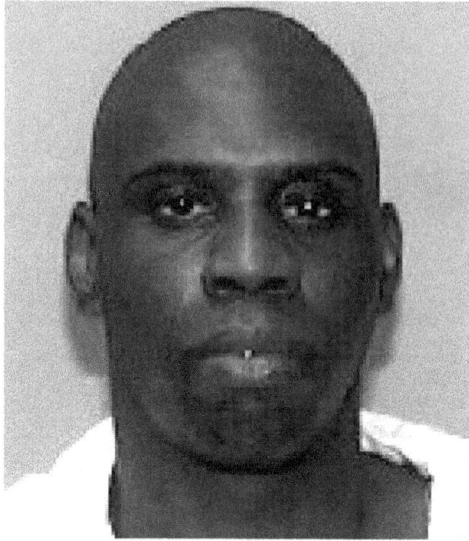

#495 Ronnie Threadgill / April 16, 2013

"I am going to a better place."

I can think of no more depressing of a place to be than lying on a gurney and waiting to die. With the executioners swarming, Ronnie Threadgill wanted everyone to know that he was going to a better place. How often do we live our lives consumed with all of the morbid and depressing shit going on all around us and forget that we are going to a better place? Look to the sky my friends! God has given us the ability to imagine the fruition of all our hopes and dreams for a reason.

No matter what you are going through, I invite you to pray the last words of Ronnie Threadgill:

"I am going to a better place."

Amen.

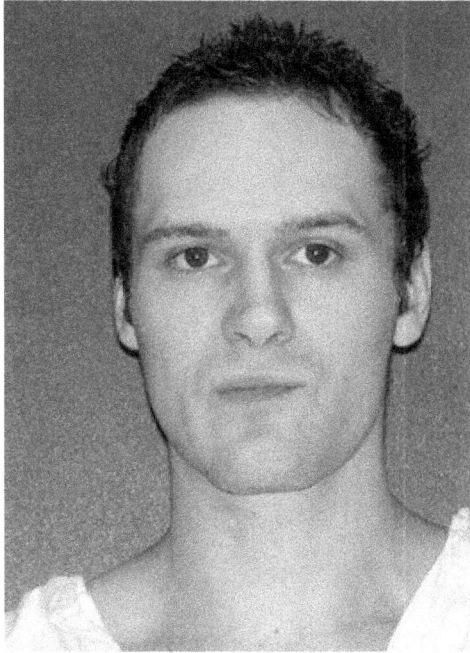

#496 Richard Cobb / April 25, 2013

"Life is death, death is life."

Matter is never created or destroyed. So what happens when we die? With the needle in his arm, Richard Cobb declared that there is life in death. The matter of Cobb or us will never created or destroyed. Life never dies.

In the juxtaposition of your daily striving, I invite you to pray the last words of Richard Cobb:

"Life is death, death is life."

Amen.

#497 Carroll Parr / May 7, 2013

"I'll be back."

To believe in an afterlife is to believe that you will be back. Maybe you won't be back to the exact same spot that you left. Since death is a tragedy for most people, I doubt that most people would want to go back to the exact spot of their death. I think that the back is actually where you started. If God is love and we started in the mind of God then I guess we just collapse back into love.

I invite you to pray the last words of Carroll Parr:

"I'll be back."

Amen.

#498 Jeffrey Williams / May 15, 2013

"I ain't got no love for anyone that don't love me."

How often do you feel this way? I'm only going to love those that love me and then I will be safe. The problem is that Jesus calls us to the dangerous spaces of a reckless love for the world. With his last words, Jeffrey Williams held on to the illusion that he could control and manage love. When he met the love of God or the God whose name is love, I am sure that Williams learned that he was no longer in control.

I invite you to pray a prayer of confession using the last words of Jeffrey Williams:

"I ain't got no love for anyone that don't love me." and add forgive me.

Amen.

#499 Elroy Chester / June 12, 2013

"A lot of people say I didn't commit those murders, I really did it."

Before he gave the Warden the go ahead, Elroy Chester wanted to make sure that everyone knew that he killed a number of people. Upon hearing Chester's confession, it is easy to label him a monster and be done with it. The harder task is to see how you are like Chester. In Matthew 5:21-22, Jesus compares and equates murder and anger. How many times have you been angry?

In confession of your anger, I invite you to pray the last words of Elroy Chester:

"A lot of people say I didn't commit those murders, I really did it."

Amen.

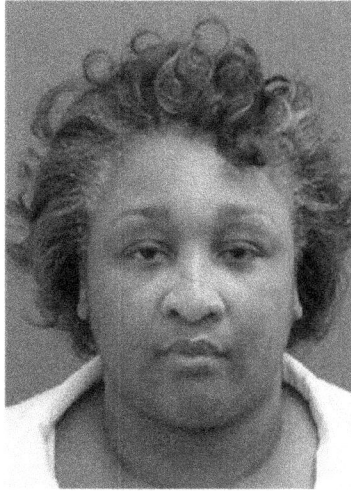

#500 Kimberly McCarthy / June 26, 2013

"I am going home to be with Jesus."

Why are we so embarrassed to talk about Jesus? We work so hard to make sure that people don't think we are too spiritual or religious in our modern age. There is something absurd about hiding love. Kimberly McCarthy was home sick for the great love of her life and the next, Jesus. Maybe we need to get a little home sick. Maybe we need to learn that love is something to be expressed and not hidden.

In anticipation of that great reunion of love, I invite you to pray the last words of Kimberly McCarthy:

"I am going home to be with Jesus."

Amen.

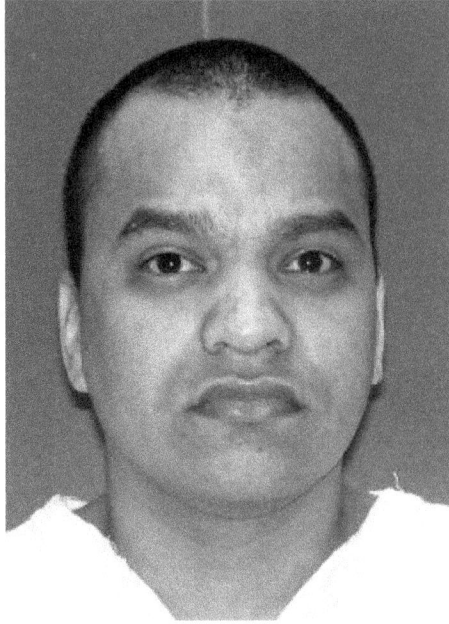

#501 John Quintanilla, Jr. / July 16, 2013

"...tell my wife that I love her..."

Who do you love? If you had a needle stuck in your arm about to pump poison through your veins, who would you express your love to one last time? John Quintanilla, Jr. wanted his wife to know how much he loved her. Though Quintanilla was executed, the love he had for his wife lives...for love never dies. Who do you love?

Thinking about the ones you love, I invite you to pray the last words of John Quintanilla, Jr.:

"...tell my wife that I love her..."

Amen.

#502 Vaughn Ross / July 18, 2013

"I don't fear death."

We are a people paralyzingly afraid of death. We are diseased with an inability to see life in death. For Vaughn Ross, life was far scarier than death. Ross was ready to depart this life for the experience of the beauty of the next. The courage of a convicted killer facing death in the execution chamber reminds us that there can be more life in dying than we could ever imagine.

I invite you to pray the last words of Vaughn Ross:

"I don't fear death."

Amen.

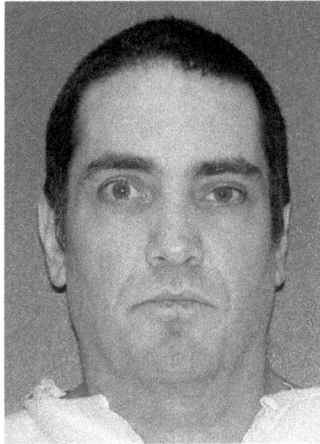

#503 Douglas Feldman / July 31, 2013

"I hereby protest my pending execution and demand
immediate relief."

Douglas Feldman was a remorseless killer. Before he uttered
his last words, Feldman declared that his killing of innocent
truck drivers were a justified death sentence that he was
forced to carry out. Why would anyone care about his last
words? Feldman protested his execution and demanded relief.
We didn't give it to him. We chose to look away in the face of a
forced death. We can do better.

I invite you to pray the last words of Douglas Feldman and
think about how you can give the next person to be executed
some relief:

"I hereby protest my pending execution and demand
immediate relief."

Amen.

#504 Robert Gaza / September 19, 2013

"It's not easy, this is a release."

Sometimes the most freeing things are the most difficult to
endure. In the hardest of moments, Robert Gaza pointed to
the the release that was upon him. I believe Gaza felt the
presence of God. One does not have to be strapped to a gurney
or lying in a hospital bed to feel like they are dying. Regardless
of your circumstance, know that God is with you and you can
always point to your release.

I invite you to pray the last words of Robert Garza:

"It's not easy, this is a release."

Amen.

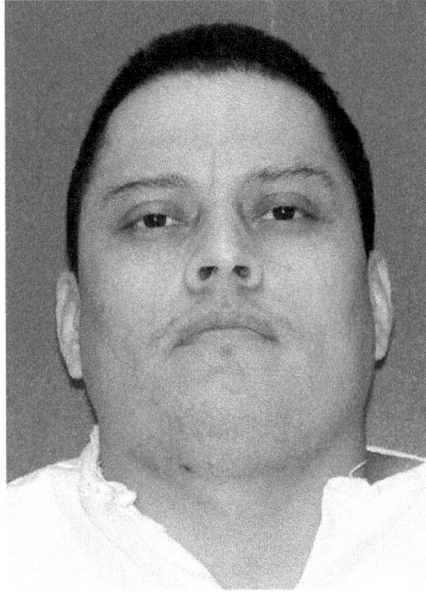

#505 Arturo Diaz/ September 26, 2013

"I have no hate for you."

Are there people out there that you simply can't stand? Do you think you could keep from hating someone who was actively trying to kill you? In the midst of a room full of his executioners, Arturo Diaz declared, "I have no hate for you." What would it look like to live your life with such grace? You can begin to find out today.

Thinking of those you despise the most, I invite you to pray the last words of Arturo Diaz:

"I have no hate for you."

Amen.

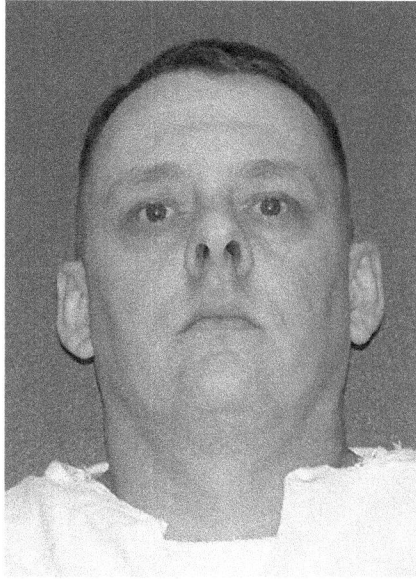

#506 Michael Yowell / October 9, 2013

"I love you."

The world is complicated. Evil and love mix on the inside and outside of every person. Michael Yowell was no different. Though he was a confessed killer, Yowell spent his final moments telling his children that he loved them. Who are we to say that the love of a killer isn't just as salvific as the love of anyone else? We spend so much time judging the love of others that we fail to live love out.

I invite you to practice love by praying the last words of Michael Yowell:

"I love you."

Amen.

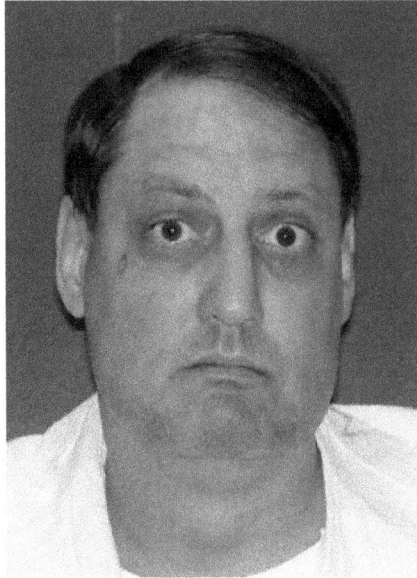

#507 Jamie McCoskey / November 12, 2013

"And if this takes the pain away, so be it."

While in the Garden of Gethsemane, Jesus kept asking God if there was any other way to take the pain away. Jamie McCoskey used similar words. There is something divine about giving our bodies to others. Though McCoskey didn't have a choice of whether or nor to die, he wanted the sacrifice of his body to mean something. We give our bodies to something daily. Why not give your body to alleviating the pain of others?

I invite pray the last words of Jamie McCoskey:

"And if this takes the pain away, so be it."

Amen.

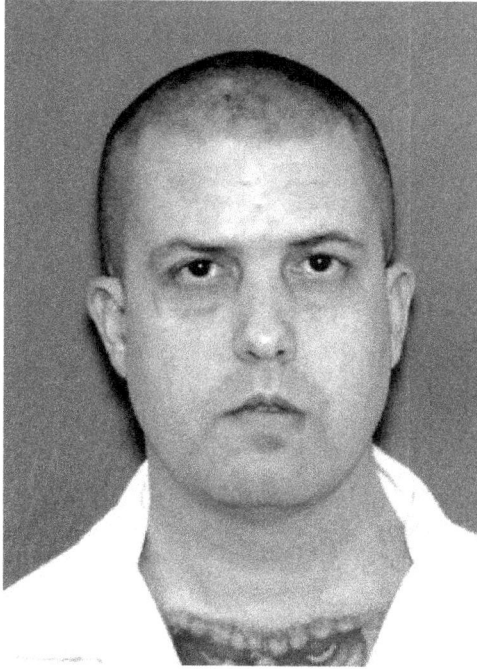

#508 Jerry Martin / December 3, 2013

"God is the ultimate judge"

Why do we worry so much about the opinions of others? If God is the judge, then none of the finite opinions floating around us matter. Our job is to please God not humanity. In his last words, Jerry Martin wanted everyone to know that he feared God more than the judgments of humanity. Do you?

I invite pray the last words of Jerry Martin:

"God is the ultimate judge"

Amen.

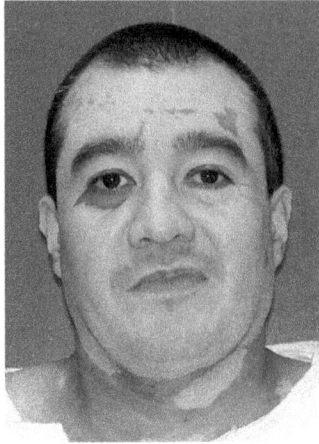

#509 Edgar Tamayo / January 22, 2014

Silence.

Mexican national Edgar Tamayo decided to remain silent during his execution. After looking back at other cases, I realized that a considerable amount of persons being executed in Texas that have remained silent are from Mexico. I have to believe that Mexicans exercising silence in the execution chamber is emblematic or an expression of the oppression faced by Mexicans throughout this country. Mexican immigrants are too often without voice or hope in the United States. Jesus calls us to do better. How can we lift up the voices and hopes of Mexican immigrants?

I invite you to ponder the plight of Mexican immigrants as you experience the lack of last words from Edgar Tamayo:

Silence.

Amen.

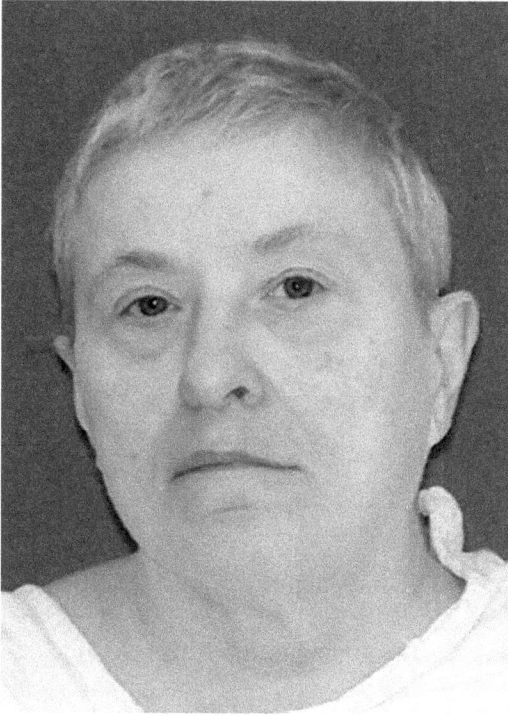

#510 Suzanne Basso / February 5, 2014

Silence.

Suzanne Basso refused to speak. Have you ever wondered why women are silenced?

I invite you to ponder the oppression of women around the world in the silence of Suzanne Basso.

Silence.

Amen.

#511 Ray Jasper / March 19, 2014

"...stay strong and faithful to God."

Sometimes we deny our own strength. Unbeknownst to us, God has placed deep reservoirs of strength within every person. Upon the culmination of many hard years on death row, Ray Jasper knew about these reservoirs. In encouraging faithfulness to God, Japer wanted everyone to know the source of his strength. For Jasper, God and strength went together. What about for you?

I invite you to pray the last words of Ray Jasper:

"...stay strong and faithful to God."

Amen.

#512 Anthony Doyle / March 27, 2014

Silence.

Anthony Doyle refused to speak in his final moments. Will we
remember the silence that we caused?

In the silence of Anthony Doyle, I invite you to experience the
silence caused by capital punishment:

Silence.

Amen.

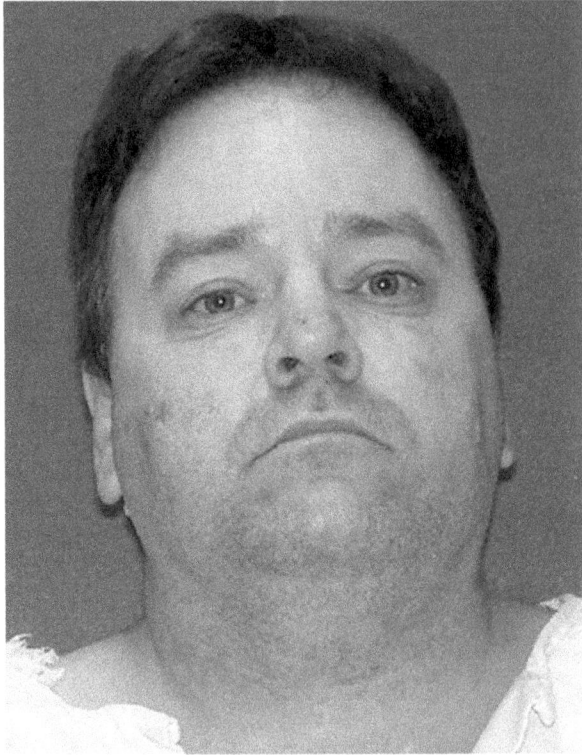

#513 Tommy Sells / April 3, 2014

Silence.

Tommy Sells was a serial killer. Do you realize this system of execution makes you one too?

In the silence of Tommy Sells, I invite you to repent:

Silence.

Amen.

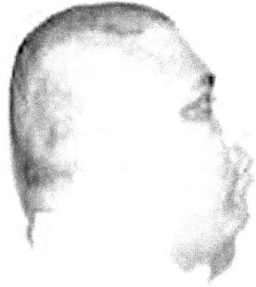

#514 Ramiro Hernandez / April 9, 2014

"All I have is love."

We go through life thinking we need so much. Unfortunately, the more we accumulate the more we think we need. People fail to realize that love will make you richer than anything else one could ever accumulate. When Ramiro Hernandez was strapped to the gurney and asked for final words, everything had been taken from him. In his last moments, Hernandez realized that love was all that he had and all that he needed. I pray that the world will learn the same lesson.

With deep understanding of just how rich you are, I invite you to pray the last words of Ramiro Hernandez:

"All I have is love."

Amen.

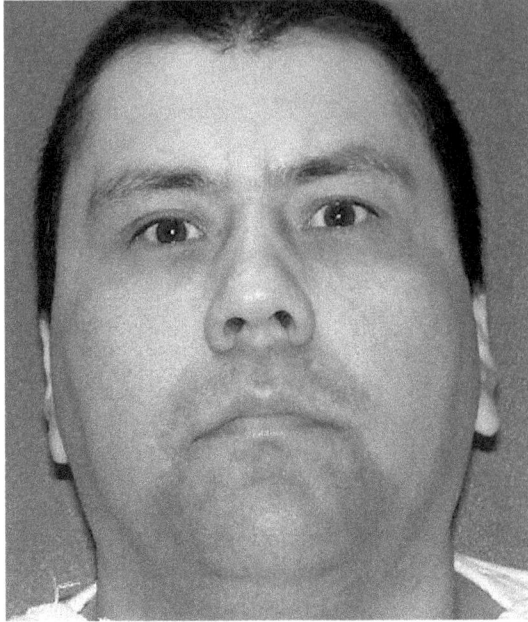

#515 Jose Villegas / April 16, 2014

"I am at peace."

In a world of violence and fear, we work so hard for peace. Unfortunately, I think that peace is far more about being and trusting than it is working. Jose Villegas understood that lesson. In his final moments, Villegas wanted the world to know that he was at peace.

After you stop working, I invite you to pray the last words of Jose Villegas:

"I am at peace."

Amen.

#516 Willie Trottie / September 10, 2014

"Find it in your hearts to forgive me."

People are desperate for forgiveness. Who do we think we are to deny them? In Matthew 6:14, Jesus taught that those who forgive will be forgiven. When Willie Trottie was about to die, he asked for people to find it in their hearts to forgive him. Who would deny a dying man forgiveness? God did not. I can promise you that.

Thinking about your own sin, I invite you to pray the last words of Willie Trottie:

"Find it in your hearts to forgive me."

Amen.

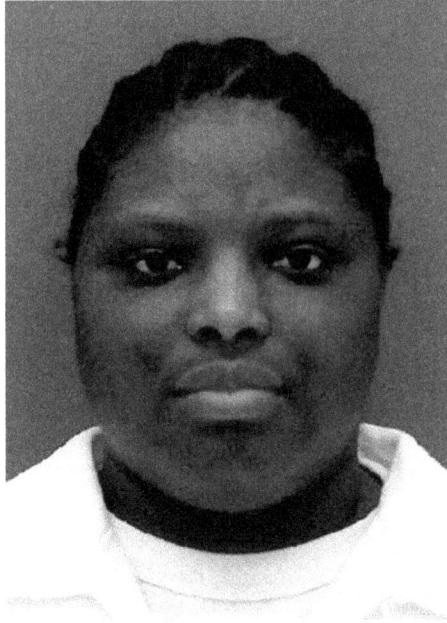

#517 Lisa Coleman / September 17, 2014

"Tell them I finished strong."

Life is about finishing strong. Do not let the failures and disappointments distract you. You are capable, but you must stay committed. Despite her circumstances, Lisa Coleman stayed committed and finished strong. I pray that we will follow her lead.

With thoughts about how you want to finish, I invite you to pray the last words of Lisa Coleman:

"Tell them I finished strong."

Amen.

#518 Miguel Angel Paredes / October 28, 2014

"I hope you let go of all of the hate because of all my actions."

How do you pray for those who hate you with good reason? When we name hate we probably make the hater hate us more. Yet, how can we not name hate for what it is. If we have been freed, how can we let anyone stay enslaved in hate? Miguel Angel Paredes knew that there were people out there who hated him and he wanted to name it before he died. We don't have to wait for death to acknowledge hate that we have caused and pray for the haters.

With the haters in mind, I invite you to pray the last words of Miguel Angel Paredes:

"I hope you let go of all of the hate because of all my actions."

Amen.

#519 Arnold Prieto / January 21, 2015

"There are no endings, only beginnings."

For Jesus, the ending was just the beginning. For Arnold Prieto, the ending was just the beginning. What about for you?

I invite you to pray the last words of Arnold Prieto:

"There are no endings, only beginnings."

Amen.

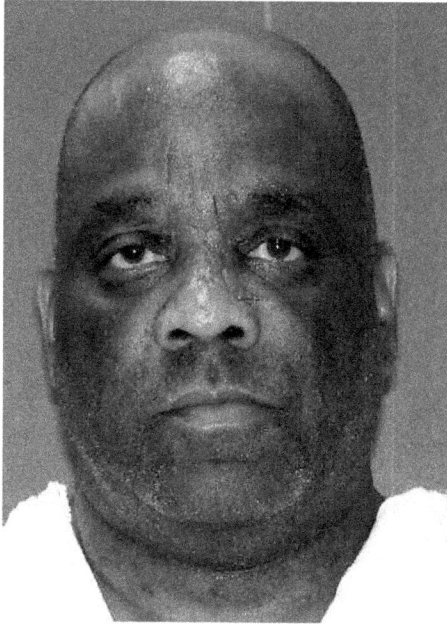

#520 Robert Ladd / January 29, 2015

"Let's ride."

We stop. We are afraid. We don't want to move an inch.
Danger is a paralyzing force. In the face of certain death,
Robert Ladd looked danger in the eye and shrugged. If we
place our trust in God, we too can have such confidence.

Staring down whatever danger you face, I invite you to pray
the last words of Robert Ladd:

"Let's ride."

Amen.

#521 Donald Newbury / February 4, 2015

"That each new indignity defeats only the body."

Donald Newbury knew that the indignity of execution could only defeat the body. For Newbury, the soul is always free for those who allow it to be. No matter the indignity of your circumstance, have you unchained your soul?

I invite you to pray the last words of **Donald Newbury**:

"That each new indignity defeats only the body."

Amen.

#522 Manuel Vasquez / March 11, 2015

"Thank you Lord for your mercy and unconditional love."

Who can describe love greater than any love imaginable? Who can comprehend love that is without end? Manuel Vasquez knew that the mercy and love of God never failed or ceased. Do you know?

I invite you to pray the last words of **Manuel Vasquez:**

"Thank you Lord for your mercy and unconditional love."

Amen.

Now, go and keep finding life in death.

Amen.

www.ingramcontent.com/pod-product-compliance
Lightning Source LLC
Chambersburg PA
CBHW060424090426
42734CB00011B/2437